Love in an Earthquake

LOVE
in an
EARTHQUAKE

by Jarold Ramsey

UNIVERSITY OF WASHINGTON PRESS

SEATTLE AND LONDON

LIBRARY OF CONGRESS CATALOGING IN PUBLICATION DATA
Ramsey, Jarold, 1937–
    Love in an earthquake.
    Poems.
    I. Title.
PS3568.A46L6   811'.5'4   72–13738
ISBN 0–295–95262–8

FOR DOROTHY

Now come with me:
The hills are steep, the day's begun,
And hearts and limbs must youthful be
To go to Oregon.

Acknowledgments

Poems in this volume have appeared previously in *The Space between Us* (London: Adam Poets, 1970) and *Shaking the Pumpkin*, ed. Jerome Rothenberg (New York: Doubleday, 1972) and in the following periodicals—*Alcheringa, The Atlantic, College English, Contempora, Doones, Fiddlehead, Laurel Review, Literary Review, The Nation, New Orleans Review, Northwest Review, Poet and Critic, Poetry Northwest, Prairie Schooner, Quarterly Review of Literature, Shenandoah, Silo, Voyages, West Coast Review.*

The following poems are workings in verse of Northwest Indian myth-texts: "How the Animals Chose Their Places," "How Her Teeth Were Pulled," "The End of the Beginning"—Isabel Kelly, "Northern Paiute Tales," *Journal of American Folklore*, vol. 51 (1938); "The Wooden Wife"—George Gibbs, "Account of Indian Mythology in Oregon and Washington Territory," ed. Ella E. Clark, *Oregon Historical Quarterly*, vol. 57 (1956); "Flathead Prophecy"—Charles Wilkes, *Narrative of the United States Exploring Expedition*, vol. 4 (New York, 1851).

The following poems included in "Songs, Games, Ceremonies" are also based on Northwest Indian myth-texts: Klamath songs—Albert Gatschet, *The Klamath Indians of Southwest Oregon*, in *Contributions to North American Ethnology*, 1890: "The Thunder Badger"—W. C. Marsden, "Notes on the Paiute Language," in University of California Publications in American Archaeology and Ethnology, vol. 20 (1920); "Girls' Game"—Melville Jacobs, *Texts in Chinook Jargon*, University of Washington Publications in Anthropology, vol. 7 (1966); "New Moon Song," "In 1852"—Melville Jacobs, *Kalapuya Texts*, University of Washington Publications in Anthropology, vol. 11 (1945); "Thunderstorm Exorcism"—Leo J. Frachtenberg, *Alsea Myths and Texts*, U.S. Bureau of American Ethnology Bulletin no. 67 (Washington, D.C., 1920).

Contents

Part 1 The Spaces between Us

Love in an Earthquake

When the big Seattle earthquake spoke
to our hill in a voice so deep our houses
bowed and scraped, you ran for the out-of-doors
but I caught you and held you bravely, me, the laird
of a home that quakes, and therefore stays, together.
Oh we had a cozy year, I guess, in the doorframe
where the Building Inspectors say always to go
and I thought I had finally saved a life
after a lifetime of trying
and perhaps if you'd been a stranger-girl
you'd have kissed me, and I'd have taken you in.

But my dear such flat heroics!
If I'd known then as I know now
your plumb heart my world turns on,
your graces that simply make it go—
I'd have let you dance right out on the rollicking
street in your dangerous joy and skip
barefooted the flipping electrical wires
and sway with our neighbors' undulant chimneys— —
I'd have seen you once at least in your earthquake freedom
with the sun jumping all over heaven for you
and the hill rolled back at your feet.

Red Cross Swimming Lesson

Trembling in sunshine before the fatal pool
by the deep end with alien children,
I felt at twelve too young to plunge and drown.
But there you were, Miss Popish, ah Miss Popish,
beckoning from the pool, your freckled bosom
gleaming wet, your shoulders streaming, and all
the rest of you mysterious under water.
Such a complicated being I
had never seen before. With an accent
I scarcely understood, you coaxed me to
the edge, and with silly knees I fell
and sank without a splash beyond your hands.
Fair teacher, now, I say this from the depths:
that fear is dry and ecstasy is wet;
if one must drown your element is best.

The Giantess on the Hillside

Thinking of you
trying to get you all in mind for praise
guessing at love against our neighbors
the pipsqueaks with their weights and measures
the words fail me, as always.

They complain, *But we were yours before you found her!*
But we have nothing for her but little paradoxes!
Proud empty-handed words.
What they won't tell of you
what crazy ways love grows to be heroic
I promise you I'll carry to a grassy hillside
west of our town, and there in full view
of every church with naked hands and feet
I'll carve the figure of an enormous woman!
She'll cover forty acres if I want her to,
and all her flesh will be grass.

First her bold mouth, grinning like an earthquake;
and then I'll run mad to work
ripping back the sod and boulders
around her head, her outflung arms,
her thighs as broad as superhighways,
feeling my way down one limb and up another
knee deep in loam until by God she's excavated,
her heathen shrines lovingly unearthed and whitewashed,
like some fabulous walled city,
my bawdy Babylon upon the hillside.

Farmers will come and solemnly pace off
her length and breadth as if this were the ritual
for seeds to swell and burst in bumper harvests,
and guides will tell them *You can see she's female*

thirty miles away in springtime. They'll say
*No one knows which god she is; there's not
a straight line in her.* Up on Mars
astronomers will tell the Press
that signs of some intelligent activity
have been observed at last on Earth,

and in our town young lovers will take heart
and lie down beneath her sheltering arms
and grown men in love will only need
to look and point, as I do now,
when the words fail them.

"And Desire Shall Fail"

—ECCLESIASTES 12

And desire shall fail
yet lovers take forever.

The greenest pine shall topple in a gale
and desire shall fail.

Triumphs every one at last grow clever
yet love might take forever.

At harvest time the locust shall prevail
and desire shall fail.

The earth must tilt and tumble off its lever,
yet lovers take forever.

My love, though desire must fail,
though bone outlasts the blood's endeavor,
yet here you lie, eager and pale,
and we shall take forever.

Forecast

Next door the fat old woman
has lost her sons to other women,
none as good as she,
her husband does not see or touch her.
I hear her warn her neighbors every day,
"It won't be long. It won't be long."
She means the frost upon her roses.

Afterward, a Soliloquy

Afterward
when we have turned away to face
our darkness down, you that way I this way,
the space between us seems like any human space
after all. After all
one plus one is one and minus one
is one and here we rest,
heavy bodies merely paired by chance of will.
I cannot guess how come we happen really
to be here, why we stay;
accomplishment means nothing now
in the gap between us, where my wristwatch
bleeds its radium out upon the sheet
and whispers to our half-lives
Prove it prove it
lead that you are

Midnight
How can my heart endure its burden of proof?
What have we made in ten good years
that in a moment would not spill and dry like blood?
You draw your knees up like a child,
like any woman: what if someone else
were falling asleep beside me in this dark
where only smooth is fair?

Then she would and I would
If she if I
But no my garish daydreams
are only lies night lies I tell myself.
And I can think of no one here but you,
only you come true beside me
with now your long fingers reaching out of sleep

to find and claim my hollow hand.
Our hands, holding, lead us through the night
like the saving children of poor parents
deaf and dumb and blind.

Child Holding a Piece of Petrified Wood against Her Bellybutton

For Sophia

Fathers will be teachers,
I teach my baby touch;
I make her feel the features
of *soft*, and *hard*, and *rough*.

I proffer her a stone,
once wood, now petrified.
"Oh, cold and hard!" we moan;
she hugs it to her hide.

Harsh against her navel
the stone's a kind of charm:
may she have no time for evil
with such a world to warm.

A child of two begins
to make me realize
salvation's in our skins—
why save them otherwise?

A Premonition

I find you here in the doorway our haven
from earthquakes   the girls beside you stunned
by sunshine   red jumpers like flags
your faces making up faces to see me
in glare coming home. And now my loves my lives
  nobody move!
Till the sun has fairly exposed us
  please nobody move

Like a Navajo sandpainting where blacklegged yellowfrocked
holy men gesture toward ripening corn
alive in flat dun fields of nothing but sand
alive   while the law in the rainbow frame keeps saying
  Your magic is strong
  but everything here
  every bright grain
  must be strewn at nightfall

Leaving for the Day

For Kate, four

When I leave our house in the morning
moping for my world, you
run and take your brave
stand behind the window
to watch me go. From
the sidewalk I turn to wave,
not wanting to, in qualms
for you my innocence.
We signal through the crazing
glass *Goodbye Goodbye*
and I am always first
to turn away and go.
I take your loss with mine,
and never dare look back
to see how solemnly
you wave until your eyes
fill up again with what
is near, and has not gone.

Threshold

Here at the door
the keys in my hand
I hoist my son John
to the height of a man
      and I feel my life go vaporing up,
      over, like the young smoke
      of a dying fire.

Looking out of the Album

The pale eyes in this photo stare south from 1910.
It is Max, and Charlcia, and the baby my mother.
What is permanent here is out-of-focus,
like the sky and old Juniper Butte hulking behind them.
They squat for the moment in stubble wearing
broad-brimmed hats and flour-sack garments.

Harvest is over, little roughnecks.

Here is Max, who has a blurred puppy under one arm;
here is Charlcia, who smirks as her grandchildren might
fencing two lolling kittens in with stubby fingers;
and here is my mother, age four, formless
as a coolie in her sackdress.
The kitten in her lap has spotted a grasshopper,
is cross-eyed, gathering to pounce! Meanwhile
my mother grins and grins doubtfully at someone
she knows standing just out of the picture.

For Lawrence Oates

Of Scott's expedition, 1912

Poor Lawrence Oates, on snowman's feet he lurched
over his comrades, dozing in their robes,
to the flap. To the smoky, windowless world
he said, *I am going outside and I may be some time.*
Forever he falters on the horizontal mountain,
nigh the Pole, black snow swirling around and over him.
For God's sake look after our people.
                                      Ah, warm friends,
you know that Oates walked out to lighten the sledge;
suppose he did it for *us*, suppose him drifting
for our sakes now weary under the world,
to ransom love in the meadows and sun for you
and me: would we still march to bring him in?
Or stay home and christen our first sons *Lawrence?*

Cain Watching Abel

For J.R.R.

I

No trail to Kinnikinnick Lake, dawn lifting
through jackstraw firs the darkness up,
up, all dead weight alive this very day!
Mist spirits move off the face of the lake
into heaven, an Indian story comes true again
over water so still it is gel, so full
of the deep night yet Narcissus the Sun
can't float his image. I find your note
snagged on a branch: MAC, CAUGHT TWO FISH,
AM GOING ON TO MERLE TO TRY THE RAFT.
SEE YOU AT NOON. IF LOST, RUN WILD.

II

Almost noon, I'm sopping with dew,
through the blowdown maze dead-reckoning
on your treed life blazing true in the wild
once more, shy brother, fugitive, pathfinder.
Your hatcheting blood cries from the higher ground.
I break out in warm sun, on open cliffs
above Merle Lake. Below in the orange
life raft you drift on your back through a field
of golden pollen, asleep on your own breath.

III

I watch for us both while a fish's splash and ripple
dances to nothing over the lake. I see the Lord
has respect to us both and what we offer,
brother, hearts drained of desire. Sin

has gone right away from the door. When the winds
come up and blow you awake, scudding
to shore, it is a kind of death I feel.
Everywhere we go from here is back.

Part 2 When Coyote Was Boss

Games, Ceremonies

'H (after Gatschet)

G OF THE SONG

e song
he song
m walking here
e song, out walking

AWK

Before the North Wind I am singing
before all the cold winds I am singing

EAGLE

Way up, way up in the sky
I make my magic circles

SONG OF THE BLIND MEDICINE GIRL

My hands flutter over the earth, searching,
they find the feathers of the yellowhammer.
I eat those feathers.

LOVERS' SONG

I have passed into womanhood,
after sunset my heart is sick.
Who comes now riding toward me?
　My little dove, fly with me!
　This way, follow me,
　before it is daylight!

How the Animals Chose Their Places

A Northern Paiute myth (after Kelly)

In the old time Coyote was boss.
Coyote said, "Bear, you better stay in the mountains."
Deer said, "I want to go live in the mountains too!"
Whitefish said, "I want some water."
Duck said he wanted water too.
Swan said, "Look at me, I am growing pretty now;
see, I am white all over."
Bear pounded the ground.
"Ground," he said, "who is talking about me?"
Ground said, "Indian talks pretty mean,"
so Bear went out and bit him.
"I want to stay here in the rocks,"
said Mountain Sheep.
"I like to feel the ground," Rock said,
"I like to stay here in one place and not move."
Sagebrush said he felt the same way.
This is Coyote's story.

How Her Teeth Were Pulled

A Northern Paiute myth (after Kelly)

In the old time women's cunts had teeth in them.
It was hard to be a man then
watching your squaw squat down to dinner
hearing the little rabbit bones crackle.
Whenever fucking was invented it died with the inventor.
If your woman said she felt like biting
    you didn't take it lightly.
maybe you just ran away to fight Numuzoho the Cannibal.

Coyote was the one who fixed things,
he fixed those toothy women!
One night he took Numuzoho's lava pestle
to bed with a mean woman
and hammer hammer crunch crunch ayi ayi
all night long—
"Husband, I am glad," she said
and all the rest is history.
To honor him we wear our necklaces of fangs.

The Wooder

Clallam (after Gibbs,

First of all there was th
he knew he was all alone
Why shouldn't I have a kin
Out in the woods he found
with the dry rot, all red an
The best he could he carved
lying down, her arms and leg
Then he shot a deer and took
its heart, tongue, and teeth, ar
in the wooden woman. *So, so,* h
Next day he killed an eagle and
and put them in the woman's hea
and began to tickle her under the
and across the breasts: she began to
That night he took the fir-woman-th
and tickled her all over until she laug
out loud, and her wooden arms and le
closed round him. *Ah, ah,* he said.
When he came back from hunting
the next night, she gave him a baby boy,
and the next night, a baby girl.

Songs,

KLAMAT

SON
I t
I t
I
th

H

COURTING SONG

Who has touched you at your secret places,
   no one?
I take you for an innocent girl
   I who have not yet lived beside you.

MOCK COURTING SONG

GIRLS: You boy, I won't love you,
     you, who run around with no blanket on.
     How could I desire such a husband!
BOYS: And I, I don't like a frog-shaped
     woman with puffy eyes!

CURSE

Shake your head
you son of a bitch
and go on south

CHINOOK (after Jacobs)

GIRLS' GAME

Let every girl go gather flowers
from marsh and meadow, hill and headland,
let one girl stand as *it*
to be draped with flowers
until it is a tree in blossom standing there
and all the others dancing quiet in a ring.
Then let her tease her friends around the ring
    Come now, look at me.
    You, your mouth is surely puckered
    You, your eyes belong to Owl
    You, your mouth is like a sturgeon's
    You, your breasts are toadstools
When someone giggles in the ring
then let her go and take her turn
as *it*, the flowering girl.

PAIUTE

THE THUNDER BADGER
Thunder-Badger lives up in the sky,
he is striped like any badger.
When the earth dries up it makes him angry,
he wants the earth to be moist.
Then he puts his head down and digs like a badger,
then the clouds come up in a flurry,
then the loud earth-cursing comes, the thunder,
then the rain comes down all over.

KALAPUYA (after Jacobs)

NEW MOON SONG
Long ago
when the new moon would come out at night
the people would speak to it, they said
New moon, we are still alive ourselves!
Here you are again new moon
little brightness
we see you — look out below!
we are still alive here yet!

ALSEA

THUNDERSTORM EXORCISM
The people would shout at Lightning
  Look sharp, jump back, my friend
  You can't hide behind me, my friend
Then the Thunder would roar,
the people would yell at him
  Look sharp, jump back, my friend
  You can't come in here, my friend

Then some would go outside and dance
and beat the house with sticks and soon
all the people would be outside dancing
and while Lightning and Thunder were leaving
one man would sing all around the house
The sky does not always act like this
The Thunder only comes sometimes
The sky is not doing anything bad
It goes right on, this world

NEZ PERCE

MORNING SPEECH
The herald rides all around the camp and sings —
It is morning!
It is morning!
I wonder if everyone is up.
We are all alive, be thankful!
Rise up! Look sharp! Go see
to the horses, maybe the wolves have killed one.
The children are alive, be thankful!
and you, older men
and you, older women
in other camps your friends are still living,
maybe, but elsewhere some are sick
this morning, and therefore their friends are sad
and therefore the children are sad.
Here, it is morning!

Flathead Prophecy Based on an Eruption of Mount St. Helens

It was fifty years ago, my whole life almost.
There were no whites to make me wonder who I am.
I whom you call Chief Cornelius of the Flatheads
was a little boy without a name
sleeping beside my mother in the lodge.
In the night my mother woke me:
Wake up! Wake up! The world is falling to pieces!
Yes, terrible thunder, the people, all of us,
crying into the dark at something darker
sifting through pine-boughs, finer than snow,
a kind of black ash ankle-deep already,
soot on our robes. I thought: Chinook Wind
will never thaw this choking winter.
But then my uncle, the medicine man you call him,
rubbed a handful of ash into the fire
and spat, and said, Oh, we will live all right,
until from the rising sun a different
kind of men will come, bringing a book,
and they will teach us everything,
and after that the world will fall to pieces.

In 1852

A Kalapuya prophecy (after Jacobs)

In the old time, by the forks of the Santiam,
a Kalapuya man lay down in an alder-grove
and dreamed his farthest dream. When he woke in the night
he told the people, "This earth beneath us
was all black, all black in my dream!"
No man could say what it meant,
that dream of our greening earth, our mother.
We forgot. But then the white men came,
those iron farmers, and we saw them plow up the ground,
the camas meadows, the little prairies by the Santiam,
and we knew we would enter their dream
of the earth plowed black forever.

The End of the Beginning

From the Paiute creation myth (after Kelly)

They are the first people.
Their children, two boys and two girls,
bicker and fight until he says to them
Go somewhere else and fight
Go in pairs you two and you two
Go different directions the rest of your lives
  Night after night he sees their campfires
burning till dawn below on the prairie,
one light to the north one light to the south
and then they are gone.
  Next morning he says to his wife
Stay here alone I am going now
When you die follow me
At the edge of the ocean she sees
him climb up on the water as if it were ice
and walk away out of her sight.
  A long time she lingers on shore, crying
Hi yah hi yee hi yah hi yee
But when she dies she stands right up
on the ocean herself and looks and looks
until she sees his campfire way over west
in the sun. When she comes he bathes her feet.
When the children die at last and come
they are all together. The world does not miss them,
it is just beginning.

Part 3 Now Indians Die In Cities

The Durgan

In my family, we call it a *durgan*,
child, it proclaims our sense of injustice.
A rebuke or refusal begins it:
you whimper and cling to the obdurate knees,
then fling yourself, scolding and screaming,
trying to catch us red-handed in anger,
arching your back so we'll think we have hurt you.
The last step is holding your breath in the corner.
In my family, we call it a *durgan*;
I did it myself, child—your father!
and may join you sometime, down on the floor.

Real Estate

I say the lands of my heart's desire
the acres of ridges and lakes in my head
are being bought up in tracts by Howard Hughes
and Henry J. Kaiser: their agents tail me everywhere!

If I carry my wife to the top of No Name Peak
and we look and embrace and give it our name *Mount Joy*
Mount Joy—or if I find by my lonesome
the long lost trail to Sublimity Meadows
and loll by the creekside letting the future
go in at one ear and the past go out at the other—

no matter where, a silent tall man in khaki
will appear on a ridge eyeing my paradise
taking it down on his clipboard hammering stakes
running the property lines with his tricky transit
till everything rare is canceled with crosshairs
and I know I'll never come back.

Tomorrow the bulldozers turnapulls backhoes will swarm
and after the Grand Dedication to Concrete
a copperplate plaque will be screwed to the map of my mind—
    Jarold Ramsey felt good here
    He and his wife had a joy here
    July 27, 1968

A Pilgrimage to Dirty John's

Dirty John Herdman is dead,
of acres of junk the master, sheer junk
so precious no one would dare to appraise it
where it lies like layers of Troy by the road
to Alfred, New York. Knowing full well how we give
with all our hearts "more laud to gilded dust
than to gilt o'er-dusted," he lordly suffered his neighbors
for fifty years to build this shrine to the god
Jetsam, each family piously carting its tithe

of rat-chewed horse-collars, chamber pots, engineblocks,
gunnysacks, stuffed foxes, dome-top radios
haunted by the news, bassinets, bird-cages
sifting full of allergies, haywire cornplanters,
chiffonieres, jardinieres, kewpie dolls and hubcaps,
the stymied Model T's that brought them here—
from each house according to its means, even,
it is said, children and pets as vestals.

Now complete, inextricably interlocked like a cipher,
this Chichen Itza of Yankee Industrial Knowhow
lies dreaming of shining Ownership and Purpose,
and within his shack in the center, John Herdman's
Midas imagination no longer burns to see
the ultimate buyer arrive in a 1937
Packard hearse cut down to a pickup
and the whole mouldering midden rise
sold in the golden air, and the fields beneath
burst into chicory and hollyhocks!

Poem for Jean Tinguely

I am haunted by all the fatigues of metal—

by the weary flexing of the Boeing's wings
      until they tuck and it drops like an anchor—
by the brave little shutters that cock and blink
      until something breaks and they stare through the exquisite
      lenses in a permanent time-exposure—
by the clattering fuel-pump in my car, overwrought, doomed—
by all motors everywhere in fact, surging
      through the night, invisibly wasting their own valves,
      rings, bearings to bright grit in the oilsumps—
by the pathos of new machines being lifted from crates,
      the terrible first turning over of moving parts—

I can't help it, I don't trust metal
but I sympathize with it deeply.

Simple hinges and nightlocks have actually
worn out in my lifetime, opening and closing;
once before marriage I dreamed that for hours in a Torture
Test I was made to screw and unscrew a bolt
      and a nut, until they lost their grip on each other
and slipped through each other like strangers—

And now I sit here under the rusty knees
      of a bridge groaning with traffic,
listening to the thin percussions of my wristwatch,
      tensing the babbitt in my joints,
sucking on a twig of copper wire.

Junior League

"In the room the women come and go,
Talking to Michelangelo."
   —Misprint in *Fourteen British and American Poets*

Beside the Durastone *David*
on Tuesday afternoon he stands,
paint on his forehead, rock-dust on his hands,
his eyes are hot and avid.
"ELIOT SENT ME—TO TELL YOU ALL!"

He's not on the Agenda,
the other lecturers look askance.
The Minister has lost his chance
to speak on Mankind's Corrigenda;
he might himself have told them all.

The ladies shun their sherbet,
and stir for questions in their tea.
"Is God dead, and Tragedy,"
asks clever Molly Hapgood Herbert,
"and Man himself about to fall?"

"THE RAINS COME, THE RAINS GO,
THE MOUNTAINS STAND, THE RIVERS FLOW,"
    says Michelangelo to the ladies,
       the ladies,
    says Michelangelo.

"THE WORLD GOES ON IN SPITE OF MAN,
WHIRLED WITHOUT END AMEN AMEN,"
    says Michelangelo to the ladies,
       the ladies,
    says Michelangelo.

"YOU WANT THE GIST OF LIFE DEFINED?
IF LIFE IS MATTER, THEN NEVER MIND.
IF MIND, NO MATTER. GOD IS KIND,"
    says Michelangelo to the ladies,
        the ladies,
    says Michelangelo.

The ladies applaud, he smirks
and vanishes. Our Molly sighs,
leans to the Minister, closes her eyes,
and whispers, "I *love* his works,
but that's not what I meant, not it at all."

And out of the lounge the ladies go
        still talking of
        talking to
Michelangelo!

Two Poets Visit a Third in Mt. Hope Cemetery

For Jonathan Williams

The gnomelike sexton tells us, riffling his register,
"Not many folks comin' round to see Adelaide
nowadays; she's Lot 7B, boys,
and just across the way's the inventor
of the Voting Machine. Oh Lordy yes,
we've got a heap of famous people here
in Mt. Hope!"

Soft rain beads the daffodils
and a blue storm comes bulging out of the south
as we find this final village of a family.
Here's Father, Mother, Sons, Wives,
Nameless Infants, bars and bars of soap—
and Adelaide in a corner,
Adelaide, who wrote her name
on two hundred pages of water, quarto.

This rain does not keep her or anybody's
measure. By the damp grave of the lady
poet, I pose and you set the focus
of your Rolleicord, and overhead in the pines
a hidden camera obscura snaps
the three of us ad infinitum.
This is our triangulation of obscurity.

For Buster Brown and Tige

Shoes are on the curbing, in the street
again, brogans, oxfords, bluchers bruised
and tumbled by the well-shod traffic
and now and then a girlish sandal gaping
for an ankle: oh vanished feet
where are you in the metal tarantella
of this city, did you cast these shoes off
blithely in the caravan of a wedding?
Or did you lose them in the THREE CAR ACCIDENT
AT MAIN AND STARK KILLS FIVE AND ORPHANS TWELVE?
Weddings
smashups
weddings smashups empty shoes intersections
so it runs
the economy of my city.

Pausing in Tonawanda

Well we spent one day in August at Niagara speechless
looking out for kegged heroes in the foam
dreaming of our lost safeties behind the cataract
then coming back at the Thruway Exit near Tonawanda

creeping forward to fling our holiday toll in the basket
we saw a big girl plump and pigtailed
stand up in the borrowpit knee deep in crass blue chicory
fall down and stand up and assault the bank to the blacktop

where she swayed for a jeopardized moment the only thing
on feet in a world of traffic then felt her way past
our front bumper as if along a narrowing ledge.
Well it was then we saw both her cheeks were dirty meat

and the pale V of her unbuttoned fly was frizzled
with sparse black tufts of her poor bush.
Her eyes and her lips were going this way and that way
ambulance flashers crying ravage ex post facto crying

O somebody what have they done with Jim Jim
Well we were next in line and had no choice in the matter
the attendant was waving us through. In the rear view mirror
we saw them wrap her up in a white towel or blanket.

Soon enough we restored the actuality of single choices
    People usually get what they want don't they
    after all in broad daylight on a superhighway
    She probably asked for it

and in two hours we were home in Rochester
watching the Special Report on Viet Nam.

The Fifth Season

Playing our game of *mind's-eye*
my child declares she sees a butterfly.
She says, "That makes it summer, right, Daddy?"
And I say, "Sure, anyway, it won't be long."
And she: "War is part of the year too, right, Daddy?"
And I: "No, war is not one of the seasons, baby!"
She opens her eyes and frowns right through me,
as well she might, she being
in her fifth winter, 1970.
War is one of our seasons.

The Meal

Here on our rug are the brutal
Indian mortar and pestle we lugged from Oregon.
You kneel and hold the mortar before you
and I pound the pestle, stone scraping stone.
Thinking the same thought we grin at each other.
Wait, squaw! let our grinding pleasure accomplish
something. See, like Moses I pour our idols
in with one hand—the brazen shrine our house,
the shards of this town with our friends
pasted between them, the flag of bandages,
the presidential dolls on a necklace,
everything in—grind! grind! grind!
round and round—we are so close
in our work our sweaty foreheads are touching.
Together we scrape up the little gray flakes
in a heap and pour in some water.
What dries in the sun
we will eat.

Part 4 To Myself in Stone

The Crow Lover

At winter dusk the bare oak branches
leaf out in black—
the crows caucus.
All day long they flap and scan
this meateating town
and now drop down
to jostle, preen, and tell each other
the worst. All night they gloat
over the dead day.

Beneath them in the oaks
I feel again the great rough joy.
My faceflesh beaks, my shoulders
are hunching into wings.
Two strokes up as the crow flies
and I'd be home.

Precision

My shadow my true reflection
if I were to lie down now
or any time on this slab of a world
arms and legs and trunk and all
I would exactly fit my shadow.
It would become me.

Eavesdropping

On the pillow of the night, black ticking
tunch tunch
tunch tunch
like a blind foot lurching
endlessly on frost. Like the stealthy tread
that crunched upon the shadows on the stair
but never caught me there. Of all the noises
underneath this terrifies me most,
echoed from my ear against the pillow—
the slow internal trudging to a halt.

Why should the heart's old cadence make me fearful,
overhearing now before the darkest dark?
Not the chance of trip or stumble
falling down
but the blind and bloody doing
private going
heedless, is what tilts my nights on edge,
throws my mind upon its downward ear.
The old hearts, sullen: they are there
to tell us we're in time to go nowhere.

Intimations

I

Evening has flown over our street
and back and found a roost: lights on.
The gaunt old man airing his Labrador
who paused to talk has moseyed on,
leashed to shadows. He asked my daughters' names,
their ages, and then stared past us down the street
the darkening way he'd come, and said
as if it should but doesn't make a world
of difference, *Ah well son*
you're in the best days of your whole life.

II

I sit here holding my sleepy kids and think years back
the brightening way I came, to a desert cemetery
in Oregon: on Memorial Day
kneeling with my mother and father to plant
cut tulips, lilacs, flags in mason jars
we'd buried at the heads of dry graves.
In a tree somewhere below the gray hill
a mourning dove is moaning for the dead.
Beyond the gatepost dustdevils whirl,
rush, and lift into the vacant sky.
From Grandmother's mounded grave under the junipers
we rise to leave, having done what rites we can,
having kept death in the family,
but someone speaks: it is the old tall woman
in black, the chalk-faced cemetery witch,
who now as always runs and takes
my young mother in her mantis arms
and madly cries *Oh child you're looking like*
your poor dead mama more with every year!

III

It is full night. The lilac-sweetened wind
blows up and down our street in search of dust.
I sit here merely holding on and think
of my kids without me. It could be.
More with every year the best days blur.
My life is an easy subtraction,
see, puff! and I'm gone.

Thaw

The tips of pines
coiled back beneath the old snow
all winter long
sprang up at me:
the dead springing up all around
all around
as I passed in the thaw.

The New Pompeii

In stone he lies, the man of Pompeii,
nameless, all but faceless, prone;
the tourists come, and eye in wonder
their calcified brother lying there.
They have questions for the guide:
"He could have fled?"
                              "Possessions held him."
"Why does he strain so on his back?"
"An air space in the ashes, *signor*."

The tourists go to view a villa.
The sun erupts above their heads,
the dust they kick will not shake off.
They feel their shadows drag along
behind their backs on sleds of stone.

The Cairn

In a dream my friends march up the road
aligned like ceremony's children. They come
for me they come with stones to build a cairn
to what I am   honor   honor.
My crippled friend without fault casts the first stone
my bosom friend the sinner casts the next one
and makes a speech all in the best of causes   mine
saying
>Marble for the statuary in his mirror
>and red lava for his little Krakatoas
>of the heart without survivors
>and sheer rimrock etched with lichens
>orange and green his legal signature
>and sandstone meaning sandstone under pressure
>dependably itself to nothing
>and geodes full of toads and flakes of schist and shale
>and here come stragglers merely flinging gravel!

So this is what I am
My friends you have brought me to myself in stone
I stand up from hiding
The cairn is tall as any man might be
posing in the roadway
I stamp   I stare all around   I laugh   I   sally forth   I
throw myself upon the pile.

The Stone Cure

"I refute it thus. . . ."
—Dr. Johnson

Deep in his mind my father drudged
for whole words, but the hospital mutes
siphoned him off in hanging bottles.
Tirelessly his eyes worked in and out like ants.

He wanted to help me, stranger, but his hands were tied
and why weren't the other judges on his side
and where were his accusing boys
and who had the time, the time
and who had jurisdiction?

O father, reason, my first mind!
The worst you've ever thought turns commonplace;
your courtroom cage of perjurers I flee,
I flee your beaten confidential stammering.
Father, have you who gave me shops of words
to rig the world's debris now fallen beyond
their hold on things, the way they are?
You try and try to say, "I only want
what's right." The doctors go on talking mean.

Out on the street, out in the tall night air
I prowled until I found a plain stone
in a pile, black, slick around as a heel:
ran up to his room and dropped the stone
into the limp and loosening grate of his hand—
Father, I cried, here, take the world's
infallible rock heart in your farmer-fist
and squeeze it white and dry!
He gripped ahold and held and held
deep down, I tell you, stranger—
and he got well.

Before Long Absence

Out here by the cliffs
out here on this plowed ground
I pile up stones in a stack.
They wobble and grate, they do not fit
well together, their carriage is painfully
erect, they begin to look
like a man.
So. So.
I have made me a friend.
He will hold this field
and this fallow sky and all the good
places where I should be
while I am gone.

Venery

"If you're going into the woods to hunt this season, remember: you're a year older than you were last season."
—NATIONAL SAFETY COUNCIL

Up on Nimrod's lookout, sighting in,
I hear your warning, and the crosshairs swim.
Ten years older than I was last season!
Alas, the aging huntsman, he must die:
a seizure takes him, just beyond the campfire,
or a wild shot as he strides a ridge,
or that demon bird the Indians knew will sing
to him, deeper and deeper through the thicket
while the twilight gathers at his back.
His lonely chase may have no stag in view,
only hoof-prints leading to a cliff.
He must fall.
              Therefore, admonish not:
we know the end, we feel it every day,
at dusk we flinch to see the hawks descend;
and still, before the flaring of each dawn
the huntsmen rise in America, and I
will stalk my beast until I stand at bay.

Part 5 Earthquake Freedoms

Memorandum

Lunching in a dusty office, eating from a green sack,
    the taste
the taste of an apple has carried me away,
away to autumn on horseback in the hill country.
Red cattle staring in a meadow, the cheat-grass
white and stiff, and in the woodpeckered trees
    apples
apples for the grabbing, cheek or pocket sized,
crimson tasting, too wild for anything but bird or boy.
I learned in joy, and learn another way
how things will stay, and serve . . .
that homestead orchard, sixty years unpruned,
windfall dropping on the settler's grave,
to show the sweet and random bounty of the earth;
    this taste
this taste revived along my tongue, to show
how far in apple eating I can go.

What the Native Said to the Geologist

"Black is the earth-globe, one inch under"
—TED HUGHES, "Two Legends"

These were not hills at the first but the waves
and swell of the Earth Dolphin, where he played
in and out of his ocean of soils and rock, flaunting
his sleek back at God, who was busy elsewhere.

Then God noticed, and said *Let there be surface tension*,
and Man uprose to that occasion, forever after
treading the land, never giving himself to it,
while Earth Dolphin sank and sank to the bottom, darkling.

But yet, if you come to this hill at a summer
noon, and roll back this stone, and hang your head
over its socket as over a dock, *so*,
you might see unimaginably deep in earth

where a dolphin
floats upright still
muzzle turned wistfully
up to the roots of all brightness.

Dreaming of Cannons

*"Before he was mustered out in '66 and went on home to the
Valley, we buried our brass cannon near the Camp. We thought
old Chief Paulina and his braves might make trouble again
sometime, and anyways, that cannon would have been* tolerable
heavy to carry back over the mountains."

   —A member of Company A, 1st Oregon Volunteers,
stationed at Camp Polk, Oregon, during Indian uprisings in
1865–66; as told to Walter Mendenhall, as told to his
nephew Max Mendenhall, as told to *his* nephews . . .

Max, your twice-told tale of buried cannons
has unhinged me, I think of nothing else
these days, so far from home I must believe it.
I close my eyes and there we are, you and I,
next summer maybe, in a humming meadow
by the boulder-rolling creek the Indians called *Why-chus*
where those homesick shiftless troopers
caught their salmon horseback, and plinked
away at deer and varmints raiding camp.
Their unused marching ground is camouflaged
in kinnikinnick and rabbit brush
and somewhere every volunteer lies mustered out
for good or bad. Now Indians die in cities.

But Max, can you imagine it—
in the loam beneath this turf and pineduff
blind breech and muzzle, long as you or me,
a cannon lies aimed at everything!
My mind burns towards the touchhole like a fuse:
cast in Philadelphia instead of bells,
Georgia oak the wheels that hearsed it here;
they rot in Oregon, while the patient roots
keep fumbling, prying at the barrel

colder than the stones beside *Why-chus*.
Like nothing else beneath this meadow
it does not turn again to earth;
darkly spin the years along its burnished bore.

Now then Max, we dig, you there, I here.
Black loam turns gray in the sun like gunpowder,
crumbling bones and ash and flakes of charcoal
explode and sift beside the deepening crater;
and soon our shovels clang like bells; sunlight
roundly glints on brass; and Max, I see us fall
and kneel like infidels before our brazen god:
unearthed, untimed, the cannon gapes and blooms.

After the Epidemic

Old Chief Cazenove

when the devil smallpox came in ships and stole
his whole village away to Memaloose Island,
ark of the dead, and Coyote's brothers
howled across the river
the story now never to be told on a winter night
to the children, hushed, reading the fire—

Old Chief Cazenove

the good factors at Fort Vancouver
set him a place at their table
and sometimes he came and sat down and studied
until the pitying white faces went strong and Indian
and the noises in the room spoke Chinook, Chinook.
Losing so much he found the world again
as Coyote found it, gigantic, simple,
dawdling at change:
and the trappers steering by Memaloose
would hear him chanting himself the stories
that always ended *The people are coming soon*.

At Olallie Camp on the McKenzie

Mild midnight on the river
eyes seared from watching alone the campfire blaze,
flare yellow, signal to the dark, creep
to embers while the mind groping
opens to the very source of night:
last man up in camp
strangely naked and awake
I carry my clothes down through the screen of alders
and totter blindly over slick stones to the river.
It is so cold I feel the friends of my flesh
join hands and dance around heart's bonfire.
I bend over and cup the invisible waters
to chest, belly, limbs.
Off across the river a broken line of riffles
phosphoresces in the starlight.

From the far bank, *over there*, do I seem myself to glow?

Crouching with numb feet on a boulder
drying off in the slow breath of the river
somehow I feel truly I am claimed.

"Bullok Sterteth"

The fat girl blundering under the elm tree
has put on weight this winter, she'll
do for a snowman in April, the flab
of her face is glazed with staring
at afternoon snows through classroom windows—
will Spring make her buxom and bonny?
Look at that! With a ponderous hump and skip
she's thrown herself out of the muck
daylight incredibly under her feet
as she leaps for the elm
of all people and she's broken
a greening twig for herself—
she knows I saw her and now as we pass
on the sidewalk she's blushing, my fat dear
if great nature is leaping this day why not you.

The Rarefaction

Staunch atop a rind
of snow upon a lava heap
upon the forest of the land
we are. Are we?
It is the rarefaction makes me wonder.
Yes, a wraith of sulfur steam
drifts vaguely up from Crater Rock
to validate by stench our nostrils.
Yes, in all this world where only clouds
and glaciers move, an icy spider creeps
around my boot, and probes, and stays.
As if the errant little spinner
knows now his elevation, and how high
he has drifted from the ponderosa meadow
where his web would be a web, and not instead
a shred of frosty lace upon the snow.
We are indeed; we know we are because
the web is shining on the snow;
it would snare us down below.

Desire at Craig Lake

Here comes the covey of little winds
out of a thicket of spruce and over the lake
like souls of children looking for something to bother.
In gangs they scurry back and forth,
over and back, now one and now twenty,
whisking the brimming water,
streaking the mirror to heaven this lake is trying to be.
What insolent slurs on perfection
what teasing of matter by motive
and here I am stretched out on a cliff downwind,
stupid with pleasure to watch the lifeless at play.
I tell the eyes in my head there is nothing behind them
but what they are seeing, forest and lake, under skylines
so dim desire will take weeks to go and return.
Meantime, in the wide green eye of this world I hide
in a corner, little man little man never there, or hardly.
I forget the dust that I am
when the winds go skating this water all morning.

Fishing with Friends on Crooked River

Since these cliffs once sundered zig-zag and let in the sky
and the tentative new river sank to final stone
and nosed its way gravity-blind for all time to the sea,
ever since then I must have been standing right here
here on this overhang fishing my life,
leg roots spelled in a crevice
like my slow sisters the alders
divining arms sprung over the deep pool.

So easy am I, so ignored,
I must never have missed one trick of the seasons' turning,
all generations of coons and water ouzels,
the bone   leaf   bud   sweet blossom
bone again of syringa,
the lone shitepoke towing
the dark upriver each night for a banner—
Nothing will ever be lost on me here
for I am the place, here is my life midway
from the cold spring on the hill, to the sea.

Yet even now
even now somewhere upstream my friend
has slipped from his ledge and is drowning!
He glides down to my pool face down
on a pallet of froth
and disappears between two boulders.
Downriver someone is shouting. I cannot move.
All animals turn away.

A Ceremony of Falling

Out here taking the edge I let
Old Faithful the wind play its one trick
with my hat, catching it thrown into space
floating   stalling   hurling it high
back over and safe to flat ground.
Three buzzards swing in for a look.
Well buzzards, well hat, faith and good flying!
But I have come to the cliffs
for a lesson in falling.

Closer, closer, old Surefoot,
the world is nearly behind. A killer
could nudge me now right over.
My tiny shadow below waves back like a lover
vague on a bed of unthinkable scree.
Out of its depths as always my heart
says *Fall down fall down and worship*
but my hands God bless them my ignorant hands
scrape on a teetering boulder and wrench it free:
two hundred pounds of basalt like an idol,
this one human push in a million years and it goes—

the long drop unseen
the mind letting go in delight
in its own blind heaven of falling
through the wind   not yet   now   crash
on a ledge   rock speech   vaulting out huge
and entire   fire and brimstone   spinning
faster and faster   a world set free
my world going down!

All around on the thunderous rimrock now
wild men are rolling big stones to the edge
we are brothers

we chant the fall of each stone over
Hoya! Hoya!
If someone real ran out below   wide eyes
white hands held up
we would not stop.

In the Thicket

"To slay, to love—the greatest enterprises of life upon man!"
—AXEL HEYST, *Victory*

We always learn something in a thicket.
At home with you now, in the ultimate confusions
of love and death, death and love, I think
of the summer I was thirteen: skulking
with an older friend named Harold in a jungle
of scraggly lodgepole pine and fern and whatnot
going dark in the dusk by the Pacific,
bat and locust hour in that slanting limbo
between the absolutes of sea and mountain forest—

we spied a man in a clearing, with a woman.
Our fright and their lust made them luminous;
we were dumfounded by all that pale motion on the ground.
He was doing things to or with that woman
we hadn't dreamed of yet. "Should we
tell my father?" I said to Harold, *sotto voce*.
"No, let's wait and see." What more to see
I never learned, for Harold's callow throat betrayed us,
cracking up between a whisper and a squeak.

The man reared up, twisting the shadows;
before our eyes his movement and the woman's,
faceless, eloquent, swimming over
the dark earth together in circles, straightened, harkened
to us, became a final spasm of recognition,
as he grabbed a rifle up and turned and fired,
snapping off four shots like curses.
Three went wild, the last one lopped a branch off
I held in my hand.
                    When we stopped running,
on the moon-stunned beach in sight of the village
our wounds were three toenails missing between us,

and my hand was numb to the wrist, as if I'd
hammered a spike on stone. "What if he'd killed us?"
asked Harold. In the sand his foot was bleeding the answer.
"Maybe she wasn't his wife," I said,
indignant in safety, limping toward final causes.

Such naïveté! And yet my hand
twenty years older grows numb once again when I phrase
for you the question I vowed that night never
to ask my father, for fear of his begging the question:
was it love somehow
was it love that wanted us dead in the thicket?

Running Wild

"Merely surviving all that is not here."
—W. S. MERWIN, "The Wilderness"

She is poised, his lover, on the high hilltop,
more naked than a deer in a gunsight.
He has hidden their clothing in a badger's burrow,
all of her things tied up in a knot in his pants-leg.
He wants to forget about clothing.
Coming back to her now, mincing on pinecones barefoot,
on the blue air tracing her skull, her breasts, her thighs,
he wonders, *Who is it who tells us we are only human?*
A mourning dove moans far off under the hillside;
it is telling another story, nothing to do with humans.
The pine trees lean and sigh, they are loving the wind,
they are full of it; the grasses are swaying; her black hair
floats on her shoulders as she turns in the wind.

All morning long they climbed in the foothills together,
crazy with sun in their brains, and the incense
of sagebrush and juniper; the quick-witted grasshoppers
were flicking and sailing under their feet,
and the buzzards revolved in the sky like planets.
He loved her for squinting and sweating like him,
out of doors it was reason enough for loving.
He felt the weight of their marriage, the grudges,
the costumes of anger and boredom, the habits
of imperfection learned by heart indoors
slip off in the heat like excess clothing.
Soon they were traveling light: when a pheasant
burst in their path like a fear from its nest, he felt
her heart with his own once more jump up jump up.
On the high hillside, she knelt and took off her
        shoes in the shadows,
and laughed and called him wanton when he said

Everything off you and me let's run wild to the meadow.
She said *Someone below might catch us*, but then
she slipped from her clothes with the grace of a lily blooming,
and leaned up from the hill to the sky, a slender stem,
a pale mariposa, honored by sunlight.

Coming back to her now, he feels the sweet blood stirring
the length of his shy mysterious body;
he carries his nakedness up to hers the way
a child comes bearing a throbbing secret, ready
at last to tell what he only knows.
She turns now and looks at him up and down,
her eyes giving depth to the skyline falling away behind her.
Nobody else on the hill in the world is looking this way.
All of him wants to touch her at once; he envies the wind
and the sunlight and shadow, embracing but never confining.
Why must we always be only human?
To be less than we are might teach us how to be more;
on this hill we are not the lords of creation,
over these birds and deer and pines there is no dominion.
When we touch for love on this hilltop we will know
the god that is in them, he is not in man's image only.
In the shadows, her shoulders are cool to his hands, her fingers
come strong to his waist, like ivy, pulling them slowly together,
eye, breath, arm, breast, loin, and sex.
For the rest of their lives they will never forget
        how the living forest
stops its round for them now, hushing
the wind, catching the small avid voices
in silence one by one, like startled children;
pausing to take them in, these naked lovers.
On every side they feel the dark eyes watching them, waiting—
and then: the mild indifference that is nature's deepest welcome.

If you will, come in to our kingdom. For you we have waited.
A chipmunk breaks the spell with its raucous chatter,
scolding a woodpecker; the woodpecker gavels its head
on a snag; the hawk's eye blinks again for prey,
and the forest resumes its intricate turning,
taking the lovers with it. What can they do for love?
She pulls from his arms with a cry and plunges over the hilltop,
running down the slope, darting between jackpines,
hair streaming back like smoke, her white woman-flesh
jolting and flashing for joy as she runs, looking back.
Now he must catch her, he is buck and ram and stallion;
the hillside plummets away beneath him, his bare feet
gouging and slipping in pineduff, the sweet-smelling boughs
raking his chest. Faster and faster his legs
are revolving like wheels, outrunning the rest of his body,
jarring and striding out of control down the hill
after her, like gods coming down. At the edge of the meadow
by the creek running free he passes and catches her
and holds and holds her still as the hillside
whirls, and lurches, and settles to rest around them.
Here is the meadow, here is our home, she says—

though the hunters step out of the grass, grinning and pointing.

Words from a Voyage

When I come home to you
I'll speak another language, absence
the silent tutor will find me words at last
to name the blessed bric-a-brac of home
you give your youth to haunt
and harry into life in every room.
I'll never go where nothing speaks of you.

When I come home to you
I'll find a tall juniper on a hill
all silvered out with berries
and mortise a new bed for us against the trunk
of four posts the one growing in the earth
that we may lie and dream
how deep the single roots twist in all directions
in the dry soil how they wind back together
join and mount at last together
to this living trunk and fragrancy of boughs
where we will lay our heads

when I come home to you.

Indian Painting, Probably Paiute, In a Cave near Madras, Oregon

Over a trail glinting with flakes
of half-worked arrowheads, jasper, obsidian, flint,
I follow an Indian entirely to stone.
His cave clenches itself around me,
I am the eye of the cliff come back to its socket
to spy on this hillside of animals breeding and dying
and boulders losing their balance. In the cave of my mind
words form white like crystals,
What remains to be seen?
I twist to the light, but glare seals me in.

What remains? Indian, the dark at the back
of your cave stays where you left it, and cold rock walls
still bruise flesh upon bone: always we live
in between. I lie where you lay. Overhead
on the spalling sky, murky with soot,
arm's length away the elk you painted
runs on head down the color of my own blood.
You made the gory sun to shine above,
and over the sun strides a kind of man with a bow.
I lie and think of that hunt: man, elk, and sun,
tracing it over and over until your paint
seems to ooze down my fingers and wrist, and clot.
Indian, flat on your back in this cave you
made what I would, a prayer to your gods;
a sign to your people you were here
but left: I follow you into stone.